The Best of Clay Pots Vol. I

～ Contents ～

4	Techniques for Crafting Success Clay Pot Prepping & Care Sources
5	Terra Cotta Pots with Style
6	Flowerpot Cat & Watch Dog & Kitten
8	"Life is a Garden" Clay Pots
10	Stars & Stripes Planters
11	The Three Watermelons
12	Independence Elephant
15	Brick & Ivy Découpage Set
16	Bee Pot Wind Chime
17	Daisy Flowerpot with Turtle Feet
18	Carrot-Top Bunny
20	Turtle Birdbath
22	Summer Breeze Windchime
24	Flowerpot Bird Feeder
26	Lucky Ladybug Garden Chime
28	Patterns

The Best of Clay Pots
Techniques For Crafting Success

How To Transfer Patterns

Trace pattern from book. Place a sheet of transfer paper (also known as graphite paper — available at craft, fabric, and art-supply stores) on your surface. Place pattern on top of transfer paper and retrace pattern lines with a pencil. The pressure of the pencil will "transfer" the pattern lines to your surface. Use dark transfer paper for light surfaces and light transfer paper for darker surfaces.

Painting Basics

- Completion time does not include drying time.
- Squeeze small amounts of paint onto paper plate as needed.
- Paint all surfaces, unless otherwise noted.
- Use as many coats as needed for good coverage; let dry between coats and color changes.
- Clean brushes or sponges thoroughly before each color change.
- To heat set paint, iron reverse side of painted area (or cover painted area with pressing cloth and iron) for 20 seconds.

Dots: Dip paintbrush handle into paint, then touch to surface. For same size dots, reload with paint after each application.

Double-Loading: Dip one side edge of brush into first paint color, and other into second paint color. Stroke back and foth across paper plate to blend.

Dry Brush: Dip brush into paint, stroke on paper towel until almost dry.

Spatter painting: Dip stiff-bristled brush, or old toothbrush, into water-thinned paint. Holding brush 4"-5" from surface, drag thumbnail or knife across bristles. Paint consistency determines spatter size. Thinner paint makes larger spatters. Practice on paper before painting on project. Protect surrounding area with newspapers or drop cloth.

Sponge painting: Wet sponge; squeeze out excess water. Sponge should be damp, not wet. Dip into paint, then dab on paper towel to remove excess.

Dimensional painting: Prevent bubbles by turning bottle upside down and tapping gently against work surface before beginning. Always store bottles with points facing down. Hold paint tip just above surface; squeeze gently until paint begins to flow, then move tip along area to be painted. The faster the tip is moved, the thinner the line of paint.

Clay Basics

- Work on flat non-porous surface such as plastic laminate, ceramic tile, or marble pastry board. Or cover wooden board with waxed paper. Tape waxed paper in place; change as needed.
- Keep work surface, hands, and tools clean. Clean hands and tools between color changes.
- "Condition" clay after removing from packaging. Warm clay in hands or seal in airtight plastic bag and submerge in hot water for a few minutes. Knead until smooth and easy to handle.
- Roll clay into balls as directed. Use acrylic rolling pin or clay-dedicated pasta machine to flatten to required thickness. Use craft knife to cut patterns from clay, unless otherwise indicated.
- Polymer clay won't harden until baked. Cool clay pieces for 30 minutes before removing from baking sheet. Clay becomes harder and more durable as it cools.
- Bake clay in well-ventilated area. Hazardous fumes can occur if clay is baked at higher temperatures or for a longer time than recommended. Turn on exhaust fan for added safety.

Basic Supplies

Paintbrushes:
- Foam
- Flat
- Round
- Liner
- Shader
- Sponge
- Stencil

Pencil
Paper
Ruler
Scissors
Craft knife
Thick craft glue
Glue gun/glue sticks
Black fine-tip permanent marker
Container of water
Paper Plate
Paper Towels
Toothpicks
Transfer paper
Fine-grit sandpaper
Tack cloth

Sources

Binney & Smith, Inc.
(800) CRAYOLA
crayola.com

Daler-Rowney
(609) 655-5252
daler-rowney.com

DecoArt
(606) 365-3193
decoart.com

Delta Technical Coatings, Inc.
(800) 423-4135
deltacrafts.com

Duncan Enterprises (Aleene's)
(559) 291-4444.
duncancrafts.com

Eclectic Products, Inc.
693-4667

Krylon/The Sherwin-Williams Co.
(800) 797-3332
krylon.com

One & Only Creations
(707) 255 8033
oneandonlycreations.com

Pebeo of America
(802) 868-5100
pebeo.com

Polyform Products Co
(847) 427-0020
sculpey.com

Walnut Hollow
(608) 935-2341
For a retailer in your area, call (800) 950-510
walnuthollow.com

Clay Pot Prepping & Care
by Rebecca Ortinau

To avoid seeing beautifully painted clay pots peel, chip, or flake, follow these guidelines to prepare and care for them:

- Remove labels from pots; sand lightly with fine-grit sandpaper.
- Clean with mild soap in warm water; rinse well. If pots have been previously used, use a stiff bristle brush to scrub clean.
- Allow pots to dry thoroughly before beginning. Place in 250º oven for several hours to remove all moisture.
- Apply two coats of water-based sealer or artist's gesso to both inside and outside surfaces of pot. Be sure to thoroughly coat drainage hole.
- If using outdoor paints, such as Patio Paint™ by DecoArt™, sealer (or gesso) is not needed. Simply basecoat all surfaces of pot with outdoor paint according to manufacturer's instructions.
- After painting, apply two coats water-based varnish.
- Allow pots to cure for two weeks before inserting plants.
- Instead of using painted pots as planters, use "liner" pots for protection.

TERRA COTTA POTS with STYLE

MATERIALS
- Clay pots: 4" diameter with saucer, 8" diameter.
- Terra Cotta oven-bake polymer clay*.
- Clay molds*: Summer Floral (APM20), Leaf Motif (APM18).
- Translucent liquid clay*.
- Clay knife*.
- Opaline Blue porcelain paint*.

*Sculpey® Original clay, E-Z Release Push Molds, Translucent Liquid Sculpey®, and Sculpey® Super Slicer by Polyform Products Co. Porcelaine 150 paint by Pebeo of America.

by Marie Segal

Finished Sizes: pansy pot, 4" diameter; tipped pot, 8" diameter
Time: 1 hour each

INSTRUCTIONS

Follow manufacturer's instructions to condition clay. Roll ¾"-diameter snake slightly shorter than pot diameter. Press snake into mold, beginning at one end and working across; trim excess. Bend mold back to release clay; remove gently.

Apply liquid clay evenly to back of border; press onto rim. Repeat as desired to cover saucer rim or to add individual motifs to sides of pot.

Bake pot in preheated 275° oven for 30 minutes. Turn off; allow pot to cool in oven. Follow paint manufacturer's instructions to apply paint and to heat set. ♥

FLOWER POT
Cat & Watch Dog & Kitten

by Barbara Matthiessen

Finished Sizes: cat, 15" tall; kitten, 8" tall; watch dog, 15" tall
Time: less than 2 hours each

INSTRUCTIONS
(Note: Paint outside surfaces of pots. If project will be used outside, basecoat inside of pots to prevent water damage. Use photo as guide.)

1 Make the Cat. Turn pots upside down. For ears, glue one ¾" disk to top of each 2" pot, covering hole. In same way, glue 1" wooden disk to top of 5½" pot for head. Glue bottoms of ears, side-by-side, to top of head pot; let dry.

Trace and cut out patterns on page 28 and 29; cut tail as indicated.

Use foam brush to basecoat all pots and tail Patio Brick. Sponge paint pots and tail Tiger Lily Orange, allowing Patio Brick to show through. Without cleaning sponge, lightly sponge over pots and tail Sunflower Yellow. While paint is still wet, and using clean side of sponge, sponge over painted areas to blend paints.

For feet, sponge a 2½"-wide Sunflower Yellow section down one

Fig. 1

MATERIALS

General (for Cat & Kitten)
- Indoor/outdoor paints*: Tiger Lily Orange, Sunflower Yellow, Daisy Cream, Wrought Iron Black, Cloud White.
- Sea sponge.
- Clear adhesive gel*.

Cat
- Clay pots: 3¼"x4½", four; 2" diameter, two; 5½" diameter, one; 7½" diameter, one.
- Indoor/outdoor paints*: Patio Brick, Geranium Red.
- White craft foam, 6mm thick, 4"x11."
- Pink satin ribbon, 1½" wide, 1 yard.
- Flat wooden discs, 1/16" thick: ¾", two; 1", one.
- Gold bell, 1" long.

Kitten
- Clay items:
  pots: ¾" diameter, two; 3" diameter, one; 4½" diameter, one; saucers: 2¼" diameter, four.
- Foxglove Pink indoor/outdoor paint*.
- Small stencil brush.
- White craft foam, 3mm thick, 3½"x6½".
- Pink satin ribbon, ½" wide, 24" length.

Dog
- Clay pots: 3¾"x4½", four; 6½" diameter, one; 8½" diameter, one.
- Paints*: metallic acrylic Shimmering Silver; indoor/outdoor: Pinecone Brown, Daisy Cream, Wrought Iron Black, Cloud White.
- Sea sponge.
- Dk. brown craft foam, 3mm thick, 8½"x11" sheets, two.
- Black satin ribbon, 1½" wide, 22" length.
- Flat wooden disk, 1/16" thick, 1" diameter.
- Natural fiber hair*, 12 inches.
- Clear adhesive gel*.

Americana®, Dazzling Metallics™, and Patio Paints™ by DecoArt™. E-6000® Industrial-Strength Adhesive by Eclectic Products, Inc. *Fancy Fiber hair by One & Only Creations®.

---

side and on top of each 3¼"x4½" pot. Repeat using Daisy Cream. In same way as before, use clean side of sponge to blend paints. Set feet aside.

To assemble cat, place 5½" pot on top of 7½" pot. (Note: Head may be glued to body if desired.) Using Sunflower Yellow, sponge paint the following: for face, a 3½"x4½" oval on center front of head; for belly, a 3½"-wide section down center front of body; for tail, 1"-wide stripes on each side of tail.

Repeat sponge painting with Daisy Cream. In same way as feet, sponge edges of paint to blend.

Using Sunflower Yellow, sponge paint the following: for inner ears, a ¾"-wide section on center front of each ear; for back stripe, a 1¼"-wide section down center back of head and body; for side stripes (see Fig. 1), 1-½"-wide sections from center side of face toward bottom back of body, leaving about 1" between side stripes and back stripe.

Transfer face. Use shader to paint Wrought Iron Black eyes and nose. Paint tongue Geranium Red. Using handle end of paintbrush and Cloud White, paint highlight dot in each eye and highlight streak across top of nose.

Use marker to draw the following: eyebrows, whiskers, muzzle line and smile, hair lines in each ear, and toe lines. Draw a wavy/broken outline around inner ear, face, belly, side stripes, back stripe, and between tail stripes.

Place feet on flat work surface, side-by-side, with toes facing forward, forming a square. Place body on top of feet. Glue tail to center back bottom of body so tail is to one side of body.

For collar, wrap ribbon around head. Tie ribbon into a 5"-wide two-loop bow; trim ribbon ends in a "V". Sew bell to knot. Spot glue collar to head.

2 Make the Kitten Turn pots upside down. For ears, glue bottoms of ¾" pots, side-by-side, to top of 3" pot; let dry. Place head on top of 4½" pot for body. (Note: Head may be glued to body if desired.)

Trace and cut out patterns on page 28 and 29; cut tail as indicated.

Sponge paint ears, head, body, tail, and saucers for feet Tiger Lily Orange. Without cleaning sponge, repeat with Sunflower Yellow. While paint is still wet, and using clean side of sponge, sponge over painted areas to blend.

For face and belly, use Daisy Cream to sponge paint a 2"-wide section down center front of head/body, starting ¾" from top of head and ending at top of body rim. In same way, sponge paint center front of ears.

(continued on page 14)

"Life is a Garden" Clay Pots

MATERIALS

- ☐ Clay pots, one each diameter: 4½", 6", 8½", 12½". (**Quick Tip:** If planning to stack pots, check fit while purchasing.)
- ☐ Indoor/outdoor paints*: Cloud White, Wrought Iron Black, Sprout Green, Pine Green, Fern Green, Tiger Lily Orange, Blue Bell, Geranium Red, Sunflower Yellow Sunshine Yellow.
- ☐ Paintbrushes*: flat shader, Series E60, #4, #8, #20; pointed round, Series E85, #2, #5, #10; liner, Series E51, #1, 2/0.
- ☐ Compressed sponge.

*Patio Paints™ by DecoArt™. Robert Simmons Expression brushes by Daler-Rowney.

by Annie Lang
based on a concept
by Rachel Schneider

Finished Size: 4"-10¾" tall
Time: less than 6 hours

INSTRUCTIONS

Wipe pots with damp cloth to remove dust. Basecoat sides and bottoms of pots Blue Bell; do not paint rims.

Trace and cut out patterns on pages 30 and 31. Cut leaves from compressed sponge and expand in water; set aside. With pot rims down, transfer remaining patterns to center of corresponding pots.

Caterpillar
For mini pot, basecoat body Sunflower Yellow, bow tie Sprout Green, nose Geranium Red, and arms Wrought Iron Black.

Dry brush cheeks Geranium Red. Use #1 liner to paint Sunshine Yellow "fur lines" around head and body. Use 2/0 liner to paint eyes and smile Wrought Iron Black and to add Cloud White highlight lines to bow and two dots to each cheek. Use 2/0 liner to outline and add details with Wrought Iron Black. Add dots around body with Cloud White.

Butterfly
For small pot, basecoat body Wrought Iron Black, wings Tiger Lily Orange, and bow tie Sunshine Yellow.

Use 2/0 liner to paint eyes and smile Cloud White. Use #1 liner to outline wings and bow tie and add movement lines with Wrought Iron Black. Use 2/0 liner to add Cloud White highlight lines around wings and body and to add tiny highlight dot to each antennae tip.

Add dots around body with Cloud White.

Bee
For medium pot, basecoat bow tie Geranium Red, every other body stripe (beginning just below bow tie) Wrought Iron Black, and remaining stripes and face (including tongue) Sunshine Yellow. Float Cloud White around inside edges of wings for transparent look.

Paint head, arms, feet, and antennae Wrought Iron Black. Paint nose Geranium Red and inner mouth Wrought Iron Black. Dry brush cheeks Geranium Red.

Paint leaves and flower stem Sprout Green, flower center Sunflower Yellow, and petals Cloud White.

Use #1 liner and Wrought Iron Black to outline, dot eyes, paint smile, and add movement lines. Use 2/0 liner to add Cloud White highlight line down center of tummy stripes and to bow folds and center knot, to dot cheeks, and to highlight fingers, feet, and arms.

Dot background Cloud White in same way as before.

Frog
For large pot, basecoat body, tongue, and eyelids Leaf Green, eyes Cloud White, inner mouth Wrought Iron Black, and tummy area Sunflower Yellow.

To shade body, double load #20 flat brush with Leaf Green and Sprout Green; apply color around body outline and onto center bottom of extended foot.

Paint flower in same way as bee pot; use #1 liner to add Cloud White highlight to flower center.

Use #1 liner and Wrought Iron Black to paint pupils and to outline and add detail lines.

Dot background Cloud White in same way as before.

Finishing
For pot rims, use appropriate size leaf sponge to sponge Sprout Green border around pots as shown. Use #1 liner and Pine Green to loosely outline each leaf and to pull vein line down center of each leaf, connecting it with leaf that follows. Dot Cloud White accent flowers between leaves. ♥

Other Options . . .
- Paint an upright pot for a favorite plant.
- Turn pots into a fun fountain with an inexpensive, purchased pump.
- Stack two pots base to base to create a cute planter.
- Use leaf motif without critters if you prefer.

Stars & Stripes Planters

MATERIALS
- ☐ Clay pots:
  6" diameter, four;
  10" diameter, two.
- ☐ Spray paints*: White Primer, Regal Blue, True Blue, Cherry Red, Gloss White.
- ☐ Clear acrylic sealer*.
- ☐ Gold-leafing pen*.
- ☐ Self-adhesive shelf paper*.
- ☐ Wood filler.
- ☐ Low-tack masking tape, 1" wide.
- ☐ Epoxy glue.

*Spray Paints, Crystal Clear Acrylic Coating, and 18 Kt. Gold Leafing Pen by Krylon®.

by Deborah Brooks

Finished size: 20" and 24" tall
Time: 3 hours

INSTRUCTIONS

1 Assemble the planters. For short planter, glue bottoms of 10" pots together. For tall planter, glue bottoms of two 6" pots together; glue bottoms of remaining 6" pots together. Glue rims of 6" pot assemblies together. Let dry.

Fill seams with wood filler. Starting with medium-grit sandpaper and ending with fine-grit, sand off excess wood filler; wipe dust.

2 Paint the planters. Trace and cut out pattern on page 31; use photocopier to reduce or enlarge as desired. Use pattern to cut stars of various sizes from shelf paper. Set aside stars.

Except for inside bottom pot, spray planters with White Primer. Spray with Gloss White. (Note: Spray painting is done in layers. For multi-colored stars, layer star cutouts from smallest to largest. Use photo as a guide.)

For white stars, peel paper backing from stars. Press stars onto planters as desired.

For striped borders, vertically apply strips of masking tape every 1" around pot rims. Spray planters with Cherry Red; let dry. To protect rims during painting process, cover white stripes with masking tape.

For red stars, position star cutouts as desired. Spray planters with True Blue; let dry. For True Blue stars, position star cutouts as desired; spray planters, including inside of top pot with Regal Blue. Let dry.

Remove tape and stars. Outline stripes and stars with gold-leafing pen. Let dry. Apply sealer to painted surfaces; let dry. (Note: If using planter for live plants, place plants in plastic pot, then place inside of planter.) ♥

Other Options . . .
- Design your own planters by mixing and matching shapes and sizes as desired.
- Use planters indoors as well as outdoors. Paint pots in color schemes to match your home or decor.
- Try a variety of spray paints, including faux finishes and metallics.

The Three Watermelons

MATERIALS
- Clay pots, one each height: 2½", 3½", 5¼".
- Acrylic paints*: Lamp Black, Snow White, True Red, Forest Green, Olive Green.
- Acrylic sealer*.
- Red/green check homespun fabric, ⅛ yard.
- Red buttons: ⅜", 1".
- Straw hat, 2½" wide.
- Black pen*, 08 point size.

*Americana® Acrylic Paints by DecoArt™. Acrylic Crystal Clear Coating by Krylon®. Pigma® Micron

by Barbara Matthiessen

Finished Size: 11½" tall
Time: less than two hours

INSTRUCTIONS

1 Prepare and paint the pots. Basecoat rims Forest Green and remainder of pots True Red.

Cut sponge into ¾"x2" rectangle. Use sponge to paint ¾" Olive Green stripes on each rim. Spatter paint stripes Forest Green.

Trace and cut out patterns on page 31. Transfer faces. Paint eyes Lamp Black. Draw eyelashes, eyebrows, mouths, and wavy vertical accent lines between each stripe on rims with pen.

Paint ½" Black seeds randomly on medium and large pots and ¼" seeds randomly on small pot. Add White highlight dots to eyes and highlight curves on each seed. Apply two coats of sealer to pots.

2 Assemble the watermelons. Stack and glue watermelons together, one on top of the other, with the largest on bottom, medium in center, and smallest on top.

Tear 2"x14" strip from fabric. Tie strip into a 3-½" wide shoestring bow; trim ends in a V-shape. Glue bow to rim of bottom watermelon; glue large button to center of bow.

With remaining fabric, tear the following strips: 1"x20", ½"x11", and ½"x3". Tie 1"x20" strip into 2" shoestring bow above rim of middle watermelon; glue to secure. In same way, tie and glue ½"x11" strip above rim of top watermelon.

Knot remaining strip; glue to rim of hat. Glue remaining button to center of knot. Glue hat to top of top watermelon. ♥

INDEPENDENCE ELEPHANT

MATERIALS
- Clay pot, 3" tall.
- Wooden items:
  split egg, 2½" long, one;
  large flat ovals, two;
  jumbo craft sticks, four;
  disc, 2⅜" diameter, one;
  spools, ¾" long, four.
- Modeling compound*.
- Acrylic paints*:
  Bridgeport Gray, White,
  Hippo Grey, Light Ivory,
  Nightfall Blue, Bonnie
  Blue, Moroccan Red, Black.
- Matte varnish.
- American flag pick, one.

*Crayola® Model Magic® by Binney & Smith, Inc.
Ceramcoat® Acrylic Paints by Delta Technical

by Barbara Greve

Finished Size: 4½" tall
Time: 2 hours

INSTRUCTIONS

1 Make the trunk. To form trunk, roll small amount of modeling compound into ½"x3" cylinder, tapering one end. Press wide end of trunk against split egg to form elephant's head. Bend trunk to hold flag pick. Insert flag pick into trunk for fit; remove pick. Remove trunk from head. Following manufacturer's instructions, let trunk harden.

2 Paint the pot, trunk, and wooden pieces. Cut a 2⅝" length from each craft stick. Mix equal parts of Bridgeport Gray with White to make light gray; basecoat all surfaces of pot, wooden items, and trunk.

Trace and cut out patterns on page 29.

Turn pot upside down on work surface. (Note: Top of pot becomes bottom of elephant's body.) Transfer blanket top (Pattern A) to body. To transfer blanket ends, wrap Pattern B around front of body.

Paint center blanket section Bonnie Blue. Paint blanket border and stars Light Ivory. With Moraccan Red, paint stripes around blanket border. Shade inside of blanket Nitefall Blue. Outline stars and blanket border and draw broken accent lines at bottom of body with marker.

Using Fig. 1 as guide, draw tail in center back of body. Shade around elephant's head (split egg), ears (ovals), legs (craft sticks), and tail with Hippo Grey.

Using Fig. 2 as guide, paint toenails Light Ivory. Accent toenails and legs with marker. For ears, use marker to draw broken accent lines around wooden ovals. Using photo as guide, glue ears and trunk to head.

Mix two parts Moroccan Red with one part Light Ivory; dry-brush cheeks. Dot eyes Black. Glue head to body.

3 Finishing. See Fig. 3. Turn elephant upside down on work surface. Spread glue around edges of wooden disc. Insert disc into elephant so disc fits snugly.

Glue one leg to each spool. Glue spools/legs to inside of elephant, making sure toenails are visible. When glue is set, turn elephant right side up. Glue flag pick into trunk. ♥

Fig. 1

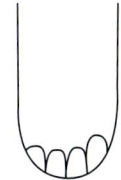
Fig. 2

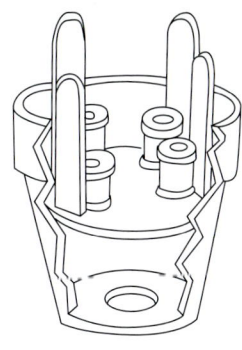
Fig. 3

Flowerpot Cat & Watch Dog & Kitten
(from page 7)

Using Sunflower Yellow, sponge paint the following: for back stripe, a ¾"-wide section down center back of head and body; for side stripes (see Fig. 1), ¾"-wide sections from center side of face toward bottom back of body, leaving ¾" between stripes and back stripe. In same way, sponge paint center top of face.

Transfer face. Dry brush cheeks Foxglove Pink. Paint eyes and nose Wrought Iron Black. Use toothpick and Cloud White to paint a highlight dot in each eye, and to paint a highlight streak across top of nose.

Use extra-fine-tip black marker to draw the following: whiskers and muzzle line; hair lines in each ear, toe lines; wavy hair lines at center top of head; wavy/broken outline around inner ear, face and belly, side stripes, back stripe, and between tail stripes.

Place feet on flat work surface, side-by-side, and toes facing forward, forming a square. Place body on top of feet. Glue tail to center back bottom of body so tail is to one side of body.

For collar, wrap ribbon around bottom of head. Tie ribbon into a 3"-wide two-loop bow; trim ribbon ends at a slant. ♥

3 Make the Watchdog
Turn pots upside down. Use foam brush to basecoat pots Cloud White. Sponge paint pots Pinecone Brown. Repeat. Mix one part Daisy Cream with two parts Pinecone Brown; sponge paint pots.

Using Daisy Cream, sponge paint the following: for face, a 3½"x5" oval, just above rim on 6½" pot; for belly, a 3" wide section down center front of 8½" pot, starting at top of body and ending just above rim.

Trace and cut out patterns on page 28 and 29. Cut materials as indicated. Transfer face to head. Use shader to paint Wrought Iron Black nose; dot eyes. Use toothpick to paint Cloud White highlight dot in eyes and highlight streak on nose.

Use marker to draw the following: eyebrows; muzzle line; freckle dots; wavy/broken outline around face, except bottom, and around belly; toe lines on 3¾"x4½" pots.

Use marker to draw wavy/broken outline around ears and tail. Cut hair in half; stack hair so ends are even. Insert hair into hole in head; glue to secure. Glue ears to head on each side of hair, so ears fall to sides of face.

Place head on body. (Note: Head may be glued to body if desired.) Place feet side by side on flat work surface, with toes facing forward, forming a square. Place body on top of feet. Glue tail to center back bottom of body so tail is to one side of body.

For dog tag, paint disk Shimmering Silver. Use marker to draw dashed outline around tag and to write name. For collar, glue ribbon around bottom of head, overlapping edges at back. **Quick Tip:** For collar, paint rim of head Wrought Iron Black, instead of using ribbon. Glue tag to center front of collar, ⅝" from top

Brick and Ivy Découpage Set

by Marcia Goss and Sue Callahan

Finished Sizes: flowerpot, 4½" tall; birdhouse, 9" tall
Time: 3 hours

INSTRUCTIONS
Basecoat pot and birdhouse base and walls Daisy Cream. Let dry.

Tear six irregular pieces of paper to mask

brick area. Use masking tape and photo as guide to attach three pieces around bottom of pot and three to birdhouse walls.

Lightly sponge paint area below pot rim and birdhouse walls Pinecone Brown. Sponge over with Daisy Cream to soften if desired.

Basecoat bottom half and roof of birdhouse with Pinecone Brown. Load sponge with Daisy Cream and Pinecone Brown; sponge paint over Pinecone Brown areas.

For brick pattern, cut a ½"x1¼" rectangle from compressed sponge. Stamp staggered Patio Brick bricks on all sides. Add a little Fern Green and/or Pinecone Brown to brick sponge and randomly accent bricks.

Remove torn paper pieces and mask outside edges with masking tape. Repeat brick pattern inside spaces. To shade openings, mix equal parts Wrought Iron Black and Pinecone Brown. Float color inside outline. Remove masking tape. Use liner brush and same mixture to paint short, crooked lines (cracks) around openings.

Cut ivy designs from napkins; separate from white paper lining. Use flat brush to cover placement area with sealer. While sealer is wet, position design, smooth with finger, and seal.
Use liner brush and basecoat color to touch up edges. Let dry. ♥

MATERIALS

- ☐ Wooden birdhouse with stand*, 9" tall.
- ☐ Clay pot, 4½" tall.
- ☐ Outdoor paints*: Pinecone Brown, Fern Green, Daisy Cream, Patio Brick, Wrought Iron Black.
- ☐ Clear sealer*.
- ☐ "Ivy on Tan" napkin*.
- ☐ Compressed sponge.
- ☐ Paper, 8"x10".

*Birdhouse by Walnut Hollow. Patio Paint®, Clear Coat Sealer, and Napkin Decor® by DecoArt™.

Bee-Pot Wind Chime

by Irene Mueller

MATERIALS

- ☐ Clay pots: 1½", one; 2½", two; 5½" one.
- ☐ Acrylic paints: yellow, black, flesh, lt. pink.
- ☐ Clear gloss varnish.
- ☐ Compressed sponge.
- ☐ Black macramé cord, 2 yards.
- ☐ Black chenille stem, 5" length.
- ☐ Wooden spools: ¾", 2".
- ☐ Raffia.
- ☐ Golf tee.
- ☐ Industrial-strength adhesive*.

*E-6000® Industrial Strength Adhesive by Eclectic Products, Inc.

Finished Size: 12" tall
Time: 2 hours

INSTRUCTIONS

Cut 1½"x2" rectangle from sponge. Sponge paint 5½" pot (body) yellow and remaining pots and golf tee (stinger) black. Apply varnish to 1½" pot, one 2½" pot, and stinger.

Using photo as guide, paint black stripes on body. Apply varnish. Paint flesh face on remaining black pot. Use black fine-tip permanent marker to draw eyes and mouth. Dry brush cheeks pink. Apply varnish.

To assemble, wrap masking tape around each cord end. Insert one cord end through ¾" spool; center spool on cord. Thread cord ends through 1½" pot from inside to outside (Fig. 1). Measure 2" from top of pot; tie a double knot.

In same way as 1½" pot, insert cord ends through 2½" pot. See Fig. 2. Insert one cord end through 2" spool; thread remaining cord end through opposite spool end. Pull cord ends so cord measures 4½" from top of 2½" pot. Tie double knots at each side of spool.

Insert cord ends through body, then head. Pull ends up so head rests on top of the body. Double knot cord at top of head so head is secured at top of body. For hanging loop, knot cord ends.

For antennae, fold chenille stem in half; curl ends as shown. Glue fold of antennae in center top of head. For bow, cut four 18" lengths from raffia; tie into 3"-wide bow. Glue bow to neck. Glue stinger to side of ¾" spool. ♥

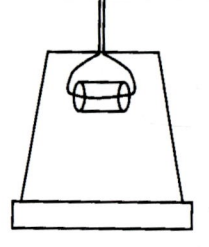

Fig. 1

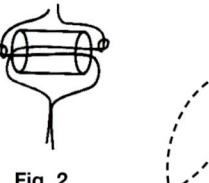

Fig. 2

DAISY FLOWERPOT with TURTLE FEET

MATERIALS
- [ ] Clay items:
  saucers: 2¼"x5" diameter, three;
  2¼"x8¾" diameter, one;
  pot: 7½"x8½" diameter.
- [ ] Wooden ball knobs, 1¾", three.
- [ ] Acrylic paints*: Lime Green, Opaque Yellow, Tangerine, White, Black.
- [ ] Clear acrylic sealer.
- [ ] Clear adhesive gel*.
- [ ] Compressed sponges.
- [ ] Black fine-tip markers: paint*; permanent.

*Ceramcoat® Acrylic Paints by Delta Technical Coatings, Inc. E-6000® Industrial-Strength Adhesive by Eclectic Products. Zig® Wood Craft Markers by EK Success Ltd.

by Barbara Matthiessen

Finished Size: 10⅜" tall
Time: less than 2 hours

INSTRUCTIONS

Turtles
Basecoat saucer (body) and ball knob (head) Lime Green. Cut a ⅜"x1" rectangle, ¾"x1⅛" rectangle, and 1" circle from compressed sponge.

Use larger rectangle sponge to paint 10 Opaque Yellow spots around shell, ½" apart, just above rim. Use smaller sponge to paint Tangerine centers.

Use round sponge to paint two Opaque Yellow feet, 1½" apart, anywhere on rim. For back feet, measure 3½" from front feet on each side; mark lightly with pencil. Sponge feet over pencil marks. (Note: Back feet will be about 2½" apart.)

Use paint marker to draw a wavy/broken outline around yellow spots, orange spots, and feet.

(Continued on page 19)

17

CARROT-TOP BUNNY

MATERIALS
- [ ] Clay pot, 4" diameter.
- [ ] Acrylic paints*: Toffee, Mink Tan, Buttermilk, Gooseberry Pink.
- [ ] Child-size ribbed orange socks, one pair.
- [ ] Green medium rickrack, two packages.
- [ ] Cotton canvas, 6" square.
- [ ] Natural burlap, 1¼"x14¼".
- [ ] Silk sunflower, 1½" diameter.
- [ ] Embroidery floss: orange, green.
- [ ] Spanish moss.
- [ ] Fiberfill stuffing.
- [ ] Orange sewing thread.

*Americana™ Acrylic Paints by DecoArt®.

by Mary Ayres

Finished Size: 8" tall
Time: 2 hours

INSTRUCTIONS

1 Paint and assemble the bunny. Basecoat outside surfaces of pot and inside rim, and both sides of canvas, Toffee. Dry brush pot and both sides of canvas Mink Tan. **Trace and cut out patterns on page 31.** Cut two ears from painted canvas.

Transfer face to front of pot so bottom of muzzle line is even with bottom of pot. Paint nose and dry brush cheeks Gooseberry Pink. Add Buttermilk highlight dot to eyes. Use black fine-tip permanent marker to draw dots on face, near nose.

Starting and ending at center back, glue burlap strip around outside rim of pot, overlapping ends. Leaving a ¼" gap between ears, glue bottom 1" of ears to inside rim of pot so gap between ears is centered over face. Glue sunflower to top of rim, between ears. Fold ears over, gluing tip of each ear to burlap with ear tips extending slightly beyond bottom edge of burlap. Use masking tape to hold ears in place until glue dries; remove tape.

2 Make the carrots. For carrots, measure and cut 5" from toe section of each sock. Discard cuff portion. Cut each toe section in half lengthwise. (Note: Each section will make two carrots.) For each carrot, turn under ¼" along cut edge; secure with straight pins. With orange thread, whipstitch edges together.

Stuff each carrot firmly with fiberfill. Fold under bottom edge of each carrot; whipstitch opening closed. To shape carrots, hold six strands of orange embroidery floss together as one. Wrap floss around top of each carrot, 1½" from end. Pull floss tightly to make indentations in carrot; knot and tie floss. Trim floss ends to ¼". Repeat four more times on each carrot at uneven intervals.

For one carrot top, wrap rickrack around 3"-wide cardboard strip seven times. Cut rickrack apart along one folded edge. With green floss, tie rickrack strands together at center. Fold in half where tied. Wrap floss around bottom of carrot top, ¼" from folded end. With green thread, sew folded end of one carrot top to center top of each carrot.

3 Finishing. To assemble, spread glue around inside of pot. Spread glue on ends of carrots. Insert ends of carrots into pot. Stuff Spanish moss around and between carrots so carrots will stand. ♥

Daisy Flowerpot with Turtle Feet
(from page 17)

For head, use Tangerine and stencil brush to dab cheeks, 1" apart, on head. Dot eyes Black. Use toothpick to paint White highlight dot in each eye and a three-dot cluster at top of each cheek. Use permanent marker to draw smile.

Glue head to body. Apply sealer. To use turtles as pot feet, place in a circle with back edges touching and heads pointing out.

Daisy Flowerpot
Trace and cut out pattern on page 31. Trace pattern onto compressed sponge; cut out. Expand sponge in water; squeeze out excess.

For saucer, sponge leaves above rim so leaves just touch at points. Use paint marker to outline leaves and to draw vein lines. Apply sealer; let dry. Paint row of leaves, outline, and draw vein lines around rim of pot in same way.

For daisies, use ruler to mark bottom of pot into quarters. Paint one leaf on each side of each quarter mark, so leaves point downward away from mark. Outline leaves with paint marker; draw vein lines.

For each flower, paint one White petal just below rim, directly above intersection of bottom leaves. Sponge paint five more petals for each flower, slightly overlapping petals. With clean sponge, paint round yellow centers.

Use paint marker to outline petals and center with a wavy/broken line. Use liner brush and Lime Green to paint stem. Apply sealer. If using pot with feet, place saucer on top of turtles; place pot in saucer. ♥

MATERIALS

- [ ] Terra cotta items:
      saucers:
      4½" diameter, four;
      6½" diameter, two;
      8" diameter, one (optional for plant holder);
      10" diameter, one;
      bowl, 11" diameter.
- [ ] Wooden ball-knobs, 1½" diameter, two.
- [ ] Acrylic paints*: Lime, Woodland Night Green, Pink Parfait, Bahama Purple, Black, White.
- [ ] Acrylic sealer*.
- [ ] Flat sponge paintbrush.
- [ ] Sponges: sea, compressed.
- [ ] Black permanent markers: fine-point, chisel point.
- [ ] Outdoor glue*.

*Ceramcoat® Acrylic Paints and Exterior Gloss Varnish by Delta Technical Coatings, Inc. E6000® Adhesive by Eclectic

by Barbara Matthiessen

Finished Size: 9¾" tall
Time: less than 3 hours

INSTRUCTIONS

1 Basecoat the pieces. Basecoat all surfaces of clay bowl, 4½" saucers and 6½" saucers Lime. Paint 10" saucer Woodland Night Green. (Optional: Basecoat 8" saucer Pink Parfait.)

Place ball-knobs, flat side down, on work surface. Draw a 1" circle on one side of each ball knob so that bottom of circle is at bottom edge of ball knob eye. Paint each circle with Black. Paint remainder of each eye Lime.

2 Paint the details. Except for one 6½" saucer, 8" saucer, and 10" saucer, turn saucers upside down on work surface.

Sponge paint outside surfaces of saucers Woodland Night Green, slightly alternating hand position with each application for a random pattern. (Optional: Lightly sponge paint entire surface of 8" saucer Lime, then Bahama Purple.)

For spots, cut one ½" circle and one 1¼" circle from compressed sponge.

Expand large circle in water; squeeze out excess. Sponge paint Pink Parfait spots, evenly spaced, around outside rim. Paint three rows of spots, with spots 2" apart, around outside of bowl. Offset each row of spots from the row below.

For remaining 6½" saucer, sponge paint four Pink Parfait spots on top of saucer. Spacing spots every 1", sponge paint one row of Pink Parfait spots around sides of saucer.

In the same way as large spots, use ¼" sponge to paint Bahama Purple spots in center of each Pink Parfait spot.

For toes, use pencil eraser and Pink Parfait to paint three spots, ½" apart, on outside rim of each 4½" saucer.

For cheeks, use sponge brush and Pink Parfait to paint a 3" diameter circle on opposite sides of sponge-painted 6½" saucer. Cheeks should extend over sides of saucer to rim and be approximately 3¾" apart at top front edge of head. Using toothpick and White, paint two highlight dots at top edge of each eye and three dots at front edge of each cheek.

Use fine-point marker to draw the following: a wavy/broken outline around each pink and purple spot; cheek and toe outlines; accent lines around front of eyes; outline rim on each foot.

For mouth, use chisel point marker. Turn marker on its side to draw a diagonal line from front edge of each cheek to bottom edge of rim; draw a line across bottom edge of rim connecting diagonal lines. Draw wavy/broken lines around outside of all pink/purple spots.

Glue eyes to top of head so that fronts of eyes are even with edge of head; let dry. Apply two coats of varnish to all painted surfaces, letting varnish dry between coats.

Using photo as assembly guide, assemble turtle. With small shell saucer upside down, glue saucer to top of bowl; let dry.

Position feet with toes facing forward and slightly outward. Place shell on top of feet so that ½" of feet extend beyond edge of shell. Place large green saucer, right side up, on top of shell. Slide back of head under front of body.

Add a few stones in bottom of birdbath; fill with water.

(Optional: If using turtle as a planter, place sponge painted pink/purple saucer, right side up, on top of shell instead of large saucer. Place plant in saucer.) ♥

Turtle Bird Bath

Summer Breeze

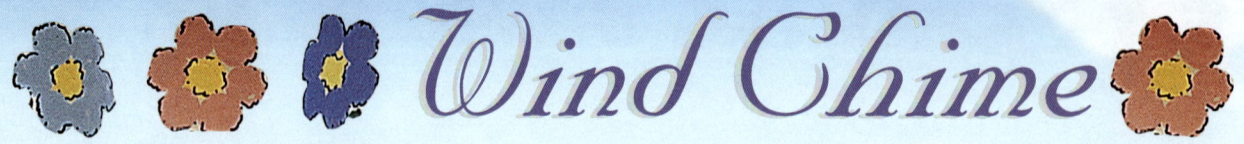
Wind Chime

MATERIALS

- [ ] Clay pots, one each diameter: 1¾", 3", 6".
- [ ] Acrylic paints: off-white, cream, pink, lavender, lt. blue, yellow, dk. green, green, red, black.
- [ ] All-purpose primer.
- [ ] Clear gloss varnish.
- [ ] Jute twine, 3-ply, 5 yards.
- [ ] Raffia.
- [ ] Wooden bead, 20mm.
- [ ] Compressed sponge.

by Irene Mueller

Finished Size: 13" long
Time: less than 2 hours

INSTRUCTIONS

1 **Prepare and paint the pots.** Apply one coat all-purpose primer to bead and all surfaces of pots. Basecoat pots off-white. Cut ⅜", ¾", and 1½" squares from compressed sponge. Use 1½" sponge to liberally sponge paint outside surfaces of pots cream.

(Note: Use photo as guide. Paint flowers on both front and back sides of each pot.) For small pot, use ⅜" sponge to paint pink checkerboard on rim. For flower, use cotton-tip swab to paint yellow dot for center and lt. blue petals. Use toothpick and green to paint stem and grass. For ladybug, add red dot to right side of flower; use toothpick to paint black center line, spots, and antennae. Use marker to draw dashed, wiggly lines around flower center and petals.

For medium pot, use ⅜" sponge to paint yellow checkerboard on rim. For flowers, dip new eraser in yellow and touch to surface of pot at center. Use eraser to paint pink petals around center. In same way, paint lavender flower on left side and lt. blue flower on right side of center flower. Use cotton swab to paint stems and grass. For ladybug, use new eraser to paint body on left side of flowers. Add details to ladybug and flowers in same way as small pot.

For large pot, use ¾" sponge to paint lt. blue checkerboard on rim. For flowers, use sponge to paint pink flower petals on pot just below center. (Note: Flower centers are sponge painted after petals on large pot.) In same way, use lavender to paint flower petals 1" from pink flower. Sponge paint yellow flower petals between pink and lavender flowers. Add yellow centers to all flowers. Use cotton-tip swab to paint dk. green stems and grass as desired. Use marker to draw dashed, wiggly lines around flower center and petals with marker.

Apply varnish to outside surfaces of all pots.

2 **Assemble the chime.** Cut three, 1-yard lengths from twine. Holding all three lengths together as one, double knot twine, 1" from end; braid twine.

Working from inside to outside, insert loose end of braid through hole in smallest pot; tie knot in braid 3" above small pot. In same way, insert braid through hole in medium pot; tie knot in braid 6½" above medium pot. Thread bead onto braid so that bead rests above knot; insert braid though hole in large pot. Tie double knot in braid above large pot, tie shoestring bow with raffia above knot.

For hanging loop, measure 15" length from top of raffia bow. Fold braid over 5" and tie a double knot; cut excess twine. ♥

Flowerpot Bird Feeder

by **Bonnie Stephens**

Finished Size: 14" tall
Time: 4 hours

MATERIALS

- [ ] Clay pots, one each diameter: 6", 8".
- [ ] Clay saucer, 10½" diameter.
- [ ] Paints*:
  acrylic: Dusty Mauve, Soft Mauve, Soft Peach, Dusty Green, Dusty Blue, Ivory, Beige, Yellow Ochre; slick dimensional: Dusty Rose, Midnight Blue, Light Brown.
- [ ] All-purpose primer*.
- [ ] Paint tips*.
- [ ] Compressed sponge.
- [ ] Flower rub-on transfers*.
- [ ] Epoxy glue.
- [ ] (Optional: Whittled birds, 5" long, two.)

*Aleene's™ Premium-Coat Acrylic Paints, Essentials™, All-Purpose Primer and Tulip® & Scribbles® 3-D Paint, Paint Tips (TL 490) and Fun Flowers Rub-on Transfers (TR 001) by Duncan Enterprises.

INSTRUCTIONS

1 Prepare and basecoat pots and saucer. Wash pots and saucer; rinse. Let dry overnight. Lightly sand outside surfaces of pots and all surfaces of saucer; wipe dust. Apply primer to outside surfaces of pots and all surfaces of saucer.

Except for rim on large pot, basecoat outside of pots Ivory. Basecoat all surfaces of saucer and rim of large pot Dusty Blue.

2 Paint and assemble the pots. Cut one 1½" square and one 1" square from compressed sponge. Set 1" sponge aside.

Wet 1½" square sponge in water to expand; squeeze out excess water until almost dry. Sponge paint Beige "bricks" every 1½" around sides of pots, leaving 1½" Ivory "bricks" in between.

In the same way as bricks, use 1" sponge to paint a row of Deep Mauve checks every 1" around rim of small pot. Paint a second row of checks above first row so that corners of checks touch.

Shade left side of each Ivory "brick" on large pot Soft Peach; shade right side of "bricks" on small pot. Spatter paint "brick" areas on each pot with Dusty Mauve.

Follow manufacturer's instructions to transfer rub-ons to sides of pot as desired. Alternating among Soft Mauve, Dusty Blue, and Soft Peach and leaving centers of flowers unpainted, paint flowers. Paint leaves Dusty Green.

(Note: Use slick dimensional paints for flower details, replacing paint caps with fine-tip liner.) Using matching dimensional paint, outline flower petals and leaves. For flower centers, alternate among dimensional colors to paint dots, swirls, or lines at each flower center. Add dots to tips of bell-shaped flowers.

Use tri-liner tip and Slick Dusty Rose to paint vertical accent lines every 1" around Dusty Blue rim. In the same way, paint lines around side of saucer below rim.

For a weathered look, lightly sand bottom edge of saucer rim and bottom edge of saucer. Apply two coats of varnish to painted surfaces. Let dry.

Center and glue bottoms of pots together. With large pot at on the bottom, glue bottom of saucer to top rim.

3 Paint the birds. Paint short-bird base Dusty Green. Paint curved surface of tall-bird base Soft Mauve; paint ends Ivory. Sponge paint short bird Beige; sponge paint tall bird Yellow Ochre, letting some Ivory basecoat show through. Thin Beige with water to an ink consistency; paint "legs." Apply varnish; let dry. Use small flat brush and Soft Peach to paint checkerboard pattern on each end of large-bird base. ♥

LUCKY LADYBUG GARDEN CHIME

by Bonnie Stephens

Finished Size: 18" tall
Time: less than 2 hours

MATERIALS

- Clay pots, one each diameter: 4½", 3⅜", 2¾".
- Wooden items*: mushroom button, ¼" diameter, one; beads, 25mm, four; apple, 2⅜" tall, one.
- Acrylic paints*: Black, True Red, White.
- Dimensional paints*: Black, White.
- All-purpose primer*.
- Satin varnish*.
- Clear adhesive gel*.
- Black craft wire: 18-gauge, 1 yard; 24-gauge, ⅔ yard.
- Artificial greenery, 6" length.
- Black satin ribbon, ⅜" wide, ⅓ yard.
- Jute twine, 3-ply, 1 yard.

*Wooden items by Lara's Crafts. Aleene's® Premium-Coat Acrylic Paint, Aleene's® Enhancers Satin Varnish and All-Purpose Primer, Tulip® 3D Paint, and Aleene's® Platinum Bond 7800 adhesive gel by Duncan Enterprises.

INSTRUCTIONS

1 Paint body and head. Follow manufacturer's instructions to apply primer to all clay and wooden items.

(Note: All pots are painted in same way. Use acrylic paint unless otherwise indicated.) For body, basecoat pot rim Black. **Quick Tip:** To ensure a smooth line, tape off pot with masking tape where it meets rim; remove tape when finished painting rim. Basecoat rest of pot, including bottom edge, True Red.

For spots, use Black dimensional paint to paint random ⅜" dots on red areas. In same way, use White dimensional paint to paint small random dots on black areas. Apply varnish; let dry.

For head, basecoat apple Black. Dot eyes White. For nose, basecoat mushroom button True Red. Glue nose to face. Apply varnish; let dry.

For antennae, basecoat beads White. Apply varnish; let dry.

2 Attach wings and antennae. Place head, bottom edge down, on scrap wood. Drill ¼" hole through center top of head, exiting at bottom. With face toward you, use tip of ⅛" bit to drill two tiny shallow holes on either side of center hole, about ⅛" from large hole.

For antennae, cut two 3" lengths from 24-gauge craft wire. Place one White bead on each wire length. Twist end around wire below bead to secure. Dip free end of wire into adhesive gel; insert free ends into shallow holes at top of head. Adjust antennae to desired position; dab with adhesive gel to secure if necessary. Set head aside.

For wings, see Fig. 1. Using 18-gauge craft wire and paint bottle for shaping, wrap wire around paint bottle to form curved wings as shown. Wings should measure 5" across; center wire stem should hang down about 2½".

To attach wings, drill three sets of holes in back of large body pot. Place body on work surface, rim down. For placement of holes, measure and lightly mark a vertical line down center of one side of pot.

Next, mark the following positions from rim with small horizontal lines: ¾" from rim; 2" from rim; 2⅞" from rim. Using ⅛" bit, drill two holes on each horizontal line, with each hole ¹⁄₁₆" from center line. Erase visible pencil lines.

To attach wings, cut three 6" lengths from 24-gauge wire. Working from inside of pot, thread each end of one length through top set of holes; repeat for remaining wire lengths. Place wire stem of wings flat against back of pot; twist 24-gauge wire lengths around stem to secure. Spot glue, if needed.

3 Assemble wind chime. Double-knot one end of twine. Thread one bead onto free end of twine. Working from inside of pot, thread twine through hole in smallest body pot. Tie remaining bead onto twine, 5" above top of smallest pot. Thread twine through hole in medium pot. Thread remaining twine through large pot and head. Double-knot end of twine into a hanging loop. Glue head to body.

4 Finishing. Glue artificial greenery around neck. With satin ribbon, tie a shoestring bow with tails; glue bow to center front of body, just below head. ♥

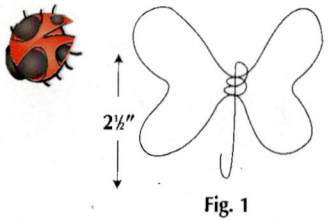

Fig. 1

FLOWERPOT CAT & WATCH DOG & KITTEN
(from page 6)

CAT TAIL
(cut 1 from white craft foam)

tape CAT TAIL pieces together

DOG FACE
(see instructions)

DOG TAIL
(cut 1 from brown craft foam)

KITTEN TAIL
(see instructions)

KITTEN FACE
(see instructions)

tape DOG TAIL pieces together

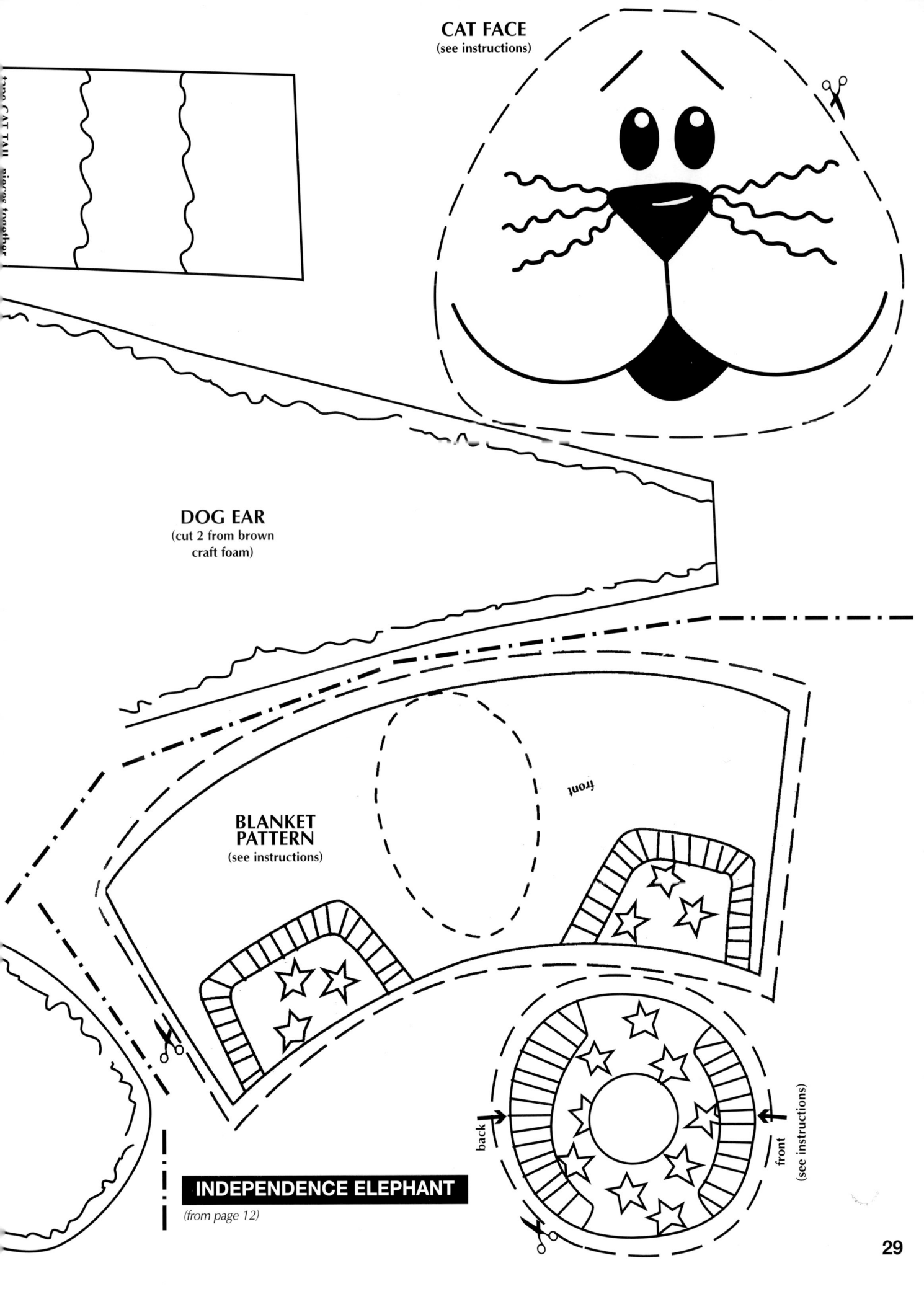